T0157518

Scribbles From God
Words to Comfort and Bless

Donna Buck Wampler

authorHOUSE®

AuthorHouse™
1663 Liberty Drive
Bloomington, IN 47403
www.authorhouse.com
Phone: 833-262-8899

© 2023 Donna Buck Wampler. All rights reserved.

No part of this book may be reproduced, stored in a retrieval system, or transmitted by any means without the written permission of the author.

Published by AuthorHouse 03/24/2023

ISBN: 979-8-8230-0422-0 (sc)
ISBN: 979-8-8230-0421-3 (e)

Print information available on the last page.

Any people depicted in stock imagery provided by Getty Images are models, and such images are being used for illustrative purposes only. Certain stock imagery © Getty Images.

This book is printed on acid-free paper.

Because of the dynamic nature of the Internet, any web addresses or links contained in this book may have changed since publication and may no longer be valid. The views expressed in this work are solely those of the author and do not necessarily reflect the views of the publisher, and the publisher hereby disclaims any responsibility for them.

Contents

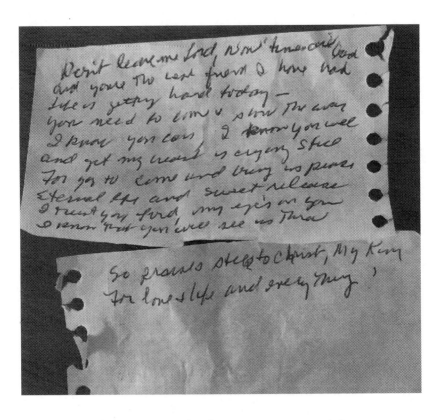

This is an example of a poem written at night
on the only scrap of paper at hand!

I call these "Scribbles from God"
because I believe He dictated them to me and I was just His
stenographer. Let me explain. I
never sat down with paper and pen
and decided to write a poem.
Instead, at the most inopportune
Times, (think middle of the middle or in
The bathtub!) the lines would come
racing to my mind, and I would grab
A pencil and paper and scribble them
down. None of them took more than
five minutes to complete, and they
needed very little polishing. So, I
give God the glory for anything you
find good here, and I am so grateful
for this fascinating gift in my life! I
believe He wanted His thoughts
shared.

The Christian Walk

As a child I heard in Sunday School
That Jesus loves me and the Golden Rule.

Then later as a teen I learned
That the ways of evil must be spurned.

Now a young woman, now a young wife,
I discovered His Word as a guide for my life.

Years later as my children grew
I found for sure He'd see me through.

With middle age came loss and grief,
Even in pain He brought relief.

Now with age what is my song?
To live what I've learned and pass it on!

Help Us See

Oh, God, You can do anything,
And do, to show us all
Your 'Happy Ending' plans for us.
Why don't we heed Your call?

You made the sun stop still for one,
Twice dried up the sea,
Revealed the future in a dream,
And saved a wretch like me!

There is no end to which You'd go
To draw the world to You—
Open our eyes so we won't miss
The many things You do.

And give us hearts that love You, Lord,
And help us clearly see
The loving plans that You have made
To win our hearts to Thee!

Gods Great Plan

God made the world, and He made man;
Our Father had a perfect plan.
But then man sinned, he disobeyed!
And God's good plans became delayed.

Generations came and went,
No single soul chose to repent,
So God devised another plan
And sent His Son to be a man.

Jesus came to pay the cost
For all the wicked, all the lost.
So choose today to be set free,
Since Jesus died for you and me,
And soon we'll live that perfect plan
That God designed when life began!

A Promise Is A Promise

Everlasting, that's the love
That You have for Your own,
Loved so much You sent Your Son,
That's how Your love was shown.

Sometimes a doubt, sometimes a fear,
Will try to steal my peace,
Then I recall these words of Yours
And I find sweet release!

Help me, Lord, to trust You more,
Believe Your every word,
For each is precious, each is true,
The sweetest I have heard.

And I am Yours and You are mine,
Forever, either way,
Whether I come home before You come
Or You call us up today!

Come Soon!

Soon You won't just stop on by,
You'll transport us up to the sky!
You'll bless, remake, and purify—
Why aren't You here? I wonder why.

Things are bad and getting worse,
We can clearly see the curse
Of sin that has so long been here.
You yearn to save us, that is clear!

So, hurry, Lord, we need
You so; It's surely near our time to go.
But may we ever more be true
And till You come, still worship You!

Holy Spirit

Holy Spirit, You're my friend,
Your care for me will never end.

You live inside, won't ever leave,
My part is simply ask, receive.

Then You will guide me all my days,
For all of this, I give You praise!

And praise the Father and the Son—
All glory to You, three in one!

Heading To Glory

God is great and God is good,
And we thank Him for our food!
But, oh my child, there's so much more
In our dear Father to adore!

He formed and made us top to toe.
He's guided us where e'er we go.
He's known and loved us from the start,
Our sadness, problems, break His heart.

He designed a plan to set us free.
Dear Jesus died for you and me,
And now we're His, His very own;
We'll see Him someday, on His throne.

For now, His Spirit lives within
To guide and keep us from our sin,
And one day it will all be o'er
And we'll know Him, like ne'er before,

A world of light and joy and love,
With all God's saved, and God above!
Hallelujah to our King—
It's now a perfect everything!

Happy Ending - New Beginning

Rapture coming, Praise His name!
For many, life won't be the same.
We'll rise in seconds - be remade—
Tickets free - Jesus paid!

Our joy will be complete in Him,
But life on earth begins to dim.
Evil comes to claim its power.
Satan has his final hour.

Then after seven years of pain
Jesus comes to earth again.
A thousand years of love and joy
For every person, girl and boy.

After that, one final test,
Then all the world is laid to rest.
Heaven comes down to cleanse the earth,
Man and planet have rebirth!

We're grateful, God, for all You've done.
We'll praise forever Your dear Son!
And worship You, our Abba, Dad,
As You complete the plan You had!

Prepared For Paradise

Born in sin I know it, Lord,
I feel the flaws in me,
And yet You promise through Your Son,
To save and set me free.

I try, sometimes do good,
Sometimes, not so much,
But You, my ever-faithful God,
Have cleansed me by Your touch.

Help me be ready, please, dear Lord,
To come at trumpet's call,
But even more, help as I wait,
To love, serve, care for all.

Make me faithful, keep me true,
Oh, let me walk with Thee
In every way You choose to lead,
Till Your sweet face I see.

Open Our Eyes, Lord

You're coming soon - You've told us so,
You've sent us signs, so we will know,
But, Lord, I need the eyes to see
The signs which You have meant for me!

There's hate and war and unbelief,
Satan ever is the thief.
Stealing peace and truth and love,
Turning some from God above.

So, Father, as I see each sign,
Seek what responsibility is mine,
Please tell me what to say and do
To prepare myself to come to You!

May I warn family and friends
There is a time when this world ends.
Please use me, Father, every day,
And when I come I'll say "Hooray!"
And may I not come all alone,
Instead bring many to Your throne!

Have You Shared?

My child, you've lived so many years
In peace and sweet content,
Knowing me and being loved,
Learning what the Bible meant.

You've taken in all that I gave,
And thanked me from the heart,
Yet do you softly hear me ask,
"Have you really done your part?"

I only ask two things from you –
Love me, and pass it on;
And you have loved and lived with me
For oh, so very long!

The greatest blessing you can find
Is sharing Calvary!
There is no greater joy in life
Than bringing souls to Me!

So spread the gospel where you live,
To each and every one,
And when at last I bring you home
You'll hear, "My child, well done!"

Friends

When times are hard, we know You're there,
We sense Your Spirit everywhere.
Angels hover near to bless,
To ease our fear, our deep distress.

But we can't see those helpers, two,
And struggle over what to do,
And then, dear Lord, You reach again,
And send in flesh, a precious friend!

It blows my mind, amazes me.
When all Your love and care I see,
That You meet every need of mine,
And send a friend who's right on time!

Thanks for friends, and family, too,
All who stand in, God, for You,
And hear, 0 Lord, my final plea,
For others, may that friend be me!

My Godly Friend

He knew you when He formed the world.
He knew your every day.
He saw your heart, within, without,
Then He smiled and said, "Okay!"

Then He saw me, and many more
Who would need a special friend,
So He knew exactly when and where
This precious gift to send!

For many years you've blessed this world,
And you have blessed me, too.
For making this, my friend, dear Lord,
The glory goes to You!

Covid Christmas

Its a far different Christmas,
A crazy old year;
But the truth is still glorious –
Jesus came that first year!

Born in a stable,
But here's the best part –
When we just say, "Welcome",
He's born in our heart!

Then everything changes;
Our loneliness ends.
For joy upon joy,
He's now our best friend!

Look Up

Oh, Lord, this world is coming apart,
As I look around, it breaks my heart!
DO NOT LOOK ON THE BITTER CUP.
LOOK UP!

But everywhere is sin and strife,
It makes me wish for a better life!
DO NOT LOOK ON THE BITTER CUP.
LOOK UP!

I see division, I see hate,
I see no way it will abate.
DO NOT LOOK ON THE BITTER CUP.
LOOK UP!

But most of all I see fear,
I don't see much that brings us cheer.
DO NOT LOOK ON THE BITTER CUP.
LOOK UP!

But since You came to rescue me,
And pay for my sins on Calvary's Tree,
And since You say, "Trust God above"
And since You pour out so much love,
I WILL NOT LOOK ON THE BITTER CUP!
I WILL LOOK UP!

My Hope

Jesus, You're my everything;
There is no hope but You.
Whatever life pours out to me
I know You'll see me through.

There's joy sometimes, but also pain,
My days are getting long,
But You are near and hold me close—
And You can keep me strong.

So I will trust You, just look up
And know You're watching me,
And one day it will all be past—
I'll forever be with Thee.

Help!

O glorious Lord, my precious Friend,
Will this time of struggle never end?
My heart's in pain, my body, too,
Dear Lord, I don't know what to do.

But I know You, You'll do it right,
So I should just give up the fight.
I know You're here, I feel Your hand,
Yet, O my God, please understand

I'm old and weak, I need Your strength,
I know You go to any length
To make me what You'd have me be.
This trial is so hard for me.

Still, I love You, You love me so.
What's right for me You surely know.
So I will trust You, bless You, too,
I know for sure You'll see me through!

Tough Times

Don't leave me Lord, now times are bad.
And You're the best friend I have had.
Life is getting hard today—
You need to come to show the way.

I know You can, I know You will,
And yet my heart is crying still
For You to come and bring us peace,
Eternal life and sweet release.

I trust You, Lord, my eye's on You,
I know that You will see us through;
So praises still to Christ, my King,
For love and life and everything!

Getting Older

Lord, I'm pretty old by now.
You got me through these years, somehow.

Some hard, some great, and some confusing,
Some even now and then amusing.

But as I'm getting near, I think,
To say farewell makes my heart sink.

And then I see, and then I know
It's way, way better when I go.

So I will keep my eyes on You
To guide me home and see me through,

And praise You daily till You call
You, dear Lord, my all in all!

Staying Strong

So now my rambling days are done,
I've found in You the perfect Son
To light my way and bring me home.
Makes me wonder, "Why'd I roam?"

You've wiped away my sinful past—
Makes me clearly want to ask,
"Why did You wait so very long?"
Now "Love to Jesus" is my song.

I have Your Spirit, so I'll stay,
In Him I can't be pulled away.
Forever Yours, my life is great,
I'll meet You soon at heaven's gate!

He Answers

O, the joy of answered prayer!
Another way You show You care.

I called You, Lord, while in great need,
You blessed me much and I was freed.

Again I prayed and asked anew,
Another pain You saw me through!

A friend in grief, a child upset,
You hear and answer- each care met.

When we don't know which way to go
We ask for guidance, then we know.

So, many thanks for answered prayer,
Your deep assurance that You care!

Trusting

I'm trusting in You, Lord,
Trusting in You,
Whatever the future
You'll see me through!

You've led me and blessed me
For all my years,
You've healed all my wounds,
Wiped away tears.

You've given me joy,
And, oh, so much more—
You poured out Your blood
Just so I could be Yours.

So I'm trusting in You, Lord,
Trusting it all—
With my hand in Yours
I never can fall.

Printed in the United States
by Baker & Taylor Publisher Services